This book is dedicated to my mom and dad for bringing me into this world and forming who I am.
Thank you to all who have helped, you know if you did...and if you didn't help, so be it.

First published in the United States of America
by Rizzoli International Publications, Inc.
300 Park Avenue South, New York, NY 10010
www.rizzoliusa.com

Big Shots

© 2017 Phillip Leeds with introduction Pharrell Williams

Book design by Bill McMullen

For Rizzoli International Publications:
Editor: Ian Luna
Project Editors: Monica Adame Davis & Meaghan McGovern
Production: Maria Pia Gramaglia & Rebecca Ambrose
Design Coordination: Kayleigh Jankowski
Proofreader: Mary Ellen Wilson

Publisher: Charles Miers

Printed in China

2017 2018 2019 2020 / 10 9 8 7 6 5 4 3 2 1
Library of Congress Control Number: 2016958875
ISBN: 978-0-7893-3264-6

PHILLIP LEEDS

BIG SHOTS!

RIZZOLI
NEW YORK

New York Paris London Milan

Children always want their parent's things. My son Theodore always wants my phone or tablet; he has his own equivalent, but wants mine. When I was young, there were no cell phones or tablets. The objects that I gravitated towards were my father's Nikon F, his stainless steel Timex, his ZERO Halliburton silver briefcase, his Polaroid SX-70. These were the coolest things I had ever seen and was not allowed to touch. This memory, along with the insane black-and-white photography collection my father has been relentlessly amassing since before I was born, is where my love of photography started. Ansel Adams, Berenice Abbott, Alfred Eisenstaedt, and Walker Evans graced the walls of my childhood home.

I never considered "being" a photographer. Despite being a very artistic kid, art, as a career choice, didn't seem to be a viable option. My father made his living as an artist manager, guiding the careers of musicians and visual artists from the '60s through the '80s. His firsthand knowledge of how difficult it is, even for the most talented artists, to gain recognition and financial success rubbed off on me. Still, I never lost the desire for that Nikon, and when I was 12, I got one for my birthday. Thus began one of my only longtime hobbies. A few years later I had the opportunity to be a photography counselor-in-training at an amazing summer camp in Connecticut called Buck's Rock. Half camper, half counselor, I learned basic darkroom techniques and became familiar with my Nikon. As I got older I really took a liking to Polaroid cameras. I loved the instant gratification of seeing if you "got the picture" within minutes of taking it and that the photo was a "one of one." In the same way the warm sounds of vinyl records, with the crackles of time and love, add character to music, the imperfections of film and the vintage camera enhance the feeling of the photos. This was way before digital cameras took instant gratification to a whole new level and made imperfections optional.

In college, my love of all things vintage and antique, which I get from my mom, took me to many garage sales and thrift stores and I began collecting vintage Polaroid cameras. Fast-forward through a lot of Polaroid 667 and 669 film to 2004, when I went to an opening for an Andy Warhol exhibition called *Warhol: Red Books*. It was a display of Andy's Polaroid portraits, in conjunction with the release of the box set of books of the same name, which replicated the way he

had kept his portraits in red Halston photo albums. At the end was Andy's Polaroid Big Shot camera, which he had used to shoot all the portraits in the show. The Big Shot is one of the most unusual-looking cameras you will ever see.

The Big Shot was made in 1971 by Polaroid, and despite being made of lightweight molded plastic, it was bulky and of limited use, as it is a fixed-focus portrait camera. With disappointing sales, it was discontinued after one year. So I went home and bought a used one off the Internet and began shooting portraits of friends who would come to my house. At the time, I was working as a tour manager for Kelis, N.E.R.D, and Pharrell. I would always travel with a lot of cameras, but the Big Shot stayed at home, being too bulky to travel with. In 2006 I stopped touring and began working for Billionaire Boys Club. I kept the Big Shot at the showroom, taking pictures of people who visited. I shot Snoop, Chris Brown, André Leon Talley, Tyler the Creator, DMC, and Jasmine Sanders at the original New York City showroom. All the while, I had *zero* aspirations for the photos beyond having them for myself. Snoop was the first person to ask me, "Why don't you have a book deal? You should definitely make a book" . . . so I asked him to be my book agent (he declined).

Several years later, in 2013, I met Ian Luna from Rizzoli. We discussed the photos and eventually began to talk about this project. It was at that moment I starting thinking about these portraits differently. Appreciating the access I had to such an amazing and extremely diverse group of people.

This book is an amazing, completely unplanned opportunity that I am truly fortunate to have stumbled into. I am constantly crossing paths with other amazing people to photograph, and this project will continue long after this book has been published. As it was in the beginning, Phillip taking pictures for Phillip.

Phillip Leeds

PHILLIP LEEDS by JONATHAN MANNION
with the POLAROID BIG SHOT

"We should take a picture of this moment."

It's so weird. So many times in life we hear a voice inside saying that. But more often than not, we fail to capture that moment.

I met Phillip way back, in '95 or '96, and he was always the guy who would say, "Let's take a picture."

He navigated a variety of circles and reliably assumed the role of crew documentarian in all of them. But not by trade as much as by circumstance: I guess you could say that he had a firm grasp of what made for that "decisive moment" because he was always right there. In his signature glasses, with a joint in one hand and a complicated vintage camera in the other—a spot-on police description of the dude responsible for all the exotic aromas that emanated from backstage at all our shows.

Maybe he had better vision than all of us.

He had a heightened perspective, a sense of elevating what seemed at the time to be an awesome but altogether inconsequential and fleeting moment. He saw in it something tangible and classic. Something not subject to differences of opinions, eroding details, or, worse, failing memories.

It's there. It is. You can hold it. You can show it to your friends and ask them: "Remember this?"

He's managed to hold on to these moments. Two decades of them. In their thousands. In tidy boxes. Pristine. Fresh. All of them framed in the way he always has.

"Phillip, you're like a photographer…"

"This book is really happening."

"Wait. Am I really writing this?"

[…]

"Phil, lemme borrow your glasses!"

—Pharrell Williams, Los Angeles, September 2016

THE ALCHEMIST

KILO KISH

14

EMORY "VEGAS" JONES

VASHTIE KOLA

DAVID ANDREW WALLACH

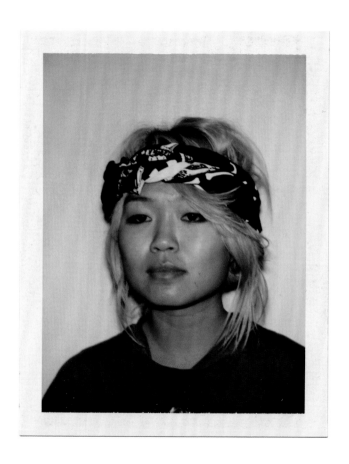

CYNTHIA LU

AHMIR KHALIB THOMPSON / ?UESTLOVE

SAMANTHA CHERTOK

MINYA QUIRK

TERRY RICHARDSON

LARGE PROFESSOR

ANTONIO SCARLATA

MIKE DEAN

KIMOU MEYER - GROTESK

DOMINIQUE TRENIER

BEN VEREEN

DJ TREATS JOEL POPOTEUR
ALL - CITY SHA NOAH SHACHTMAN

RON LAFFITTE
MARK KELLY

RHEA DUMMETT
PETER BITTENBENDER

PUSHA T

MR. ELEMENT

STRETCH ARMSTRONG

BOBBITO GARCIA

DJ CLARK KENT

LORRAINE SCHWARTZ

YOON-AMBUSH

VERBAL-AMBUSH

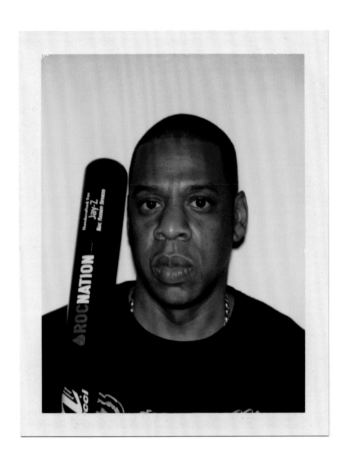

JAY Z

JAMEEL SPENCER

KID CUDI

EBRO

42

CHI MODU

CRAIG COSTELLO

RON DELSENER

RITA ORA

ROB WALKER

OFIRA SANDBERG

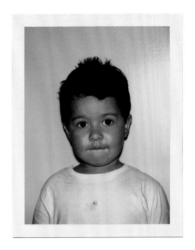

CASSELL FERERE

MYSTERY DANCER

THEODORE LEEDS

LEILA STEINBERG

TOBY FELTWELL

WAFAA NAKKOURY

WHAT THE HEC - HECTOR

BEN LEVINE

TONY ARCABASCIO

MICHAEL RAPAPORT

ROXANNE BROWN

BILL SPECTOR

ROMON YANG - ROSTARR

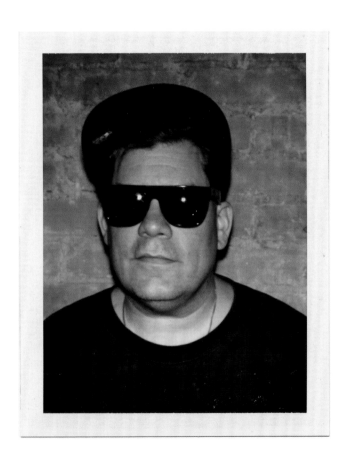

TODD JAMES - REAS

DEE JACKSON

JONATHAN MANNION

ANNE-MARIE DACYSHYN

GREG DACYSHYN

JEFF KOONS

LOUISE DONEGAN

MICK BATYSKE

HARIF GUZMAN - HACULA

MIMI VALDES　　　　　　FRANK "KNUCKLES" WALKER
P REIGN　　　　　　JERRY EDOUARD

WIM STOCKS
IBN JASPER

MASATO TAKEI
KEITH McPHEE

KOFI

DARRYL McDANIELS - DMC

68

CRAIG FORD

SUE KWON

CIPHA SOUNDS

ARI SAAL FORMAN

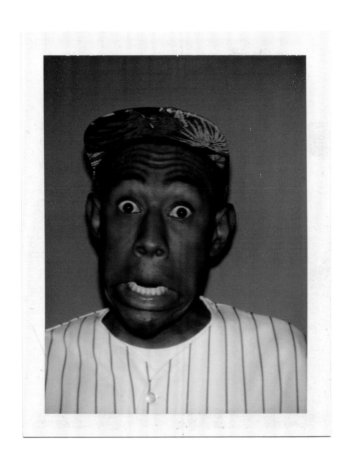

TYLER THE CREATOR

LELAND MELVIN

GOGY ESPARZA

JASMINE SANDERS

BEN EDWARDS

BRANDYNE LACKLAND

HIP HOP MIKE

JOHN JDM McPHETERS

MARK ZABLOW 40oz VAN

BRIAN STRNAD EDEN MARLEY

FAM LAY

ANDRÉ LEON TALLEY

JUSTIN TIMBERLAKE

ELI MORGAN GESNER

JADAKISS

JAY "ICEPICK" JACKSON

TED CHUNG

SNOOP DOGG

PETER LEEDS

CHRIS BROWN

FABIEN BARON

YUKI IWASHIRO

MARK McNAIRY
LITRO

VICTOR MICHAEL
ZACK KURLAND

MR. FLAWLESS

MARCUS A CLARKE

NOAH RUBIN

BUFF MONSTER

JIMMY GORECKI

ANTHONY "ANT LIVE" BARRIER

94

EMILIO ROJAS

LISA BROWNLEE

BILLIONS McMILLIONS

MACK WILDS

ANGIE MARTINEZ

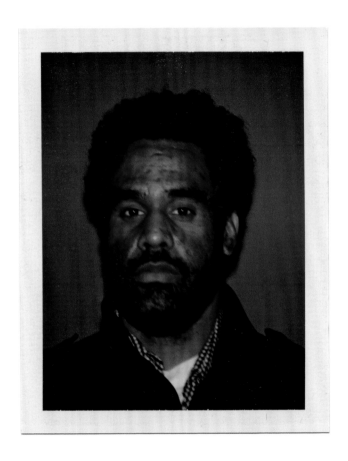

SACHA JENKINS

100

SHAE N*E*R*D

RONALD VENTURA - LEE HARVEY N*E*R*D

ROBERT GRUBMAN
ADAM SCHATZ

DILLA MAN
JOHN WAYNE

ARNAUD DELECOLLE JENNIFER DWIN & TAMMY BRAINARD
SHAHNTI O'NEILL DOMO GENESIS

PETER ROSENBERG

DEL THE FUNKY HOMOSAPIEN

106

RIFF RAFF

COLBY PARKER JR.

SZA

SCHOOLBOY Q

DANNY TREJO

CAYLA COUSINS

TARIQ TROTTER - BLACK THOUGHT

SARAH GOMES

HELEN LASICHANH

ANTONIO "NINO" SCALIA

ZEYNA SY

FRENCH MONTANA

DEXTER NAVY SLEDGREN TAYLOR GANG
DJ DIAMOND KUTS CAPTAIN KIRK DOUGLAS

GREG LaMARCHE
TUBA GOODING JR.

BIA
STEVE "ESPO" POWERS

TEYANA TAYLOR

COLTRANE CURTIS

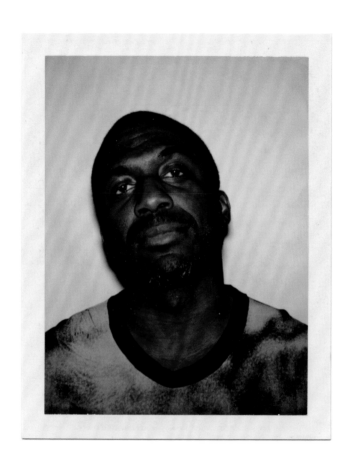

COREY SMYTH

JENN BRILL

LEFT BRAIN

JAY ELECTRONICA

VINCE STAPLES

JOHNNY CAKES

128

JELANI DAY

DAPPER DAN of HARLEM

130

CHRIS FOLKERTS

JAKE BURTON

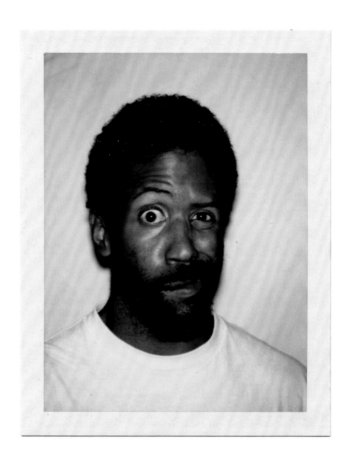

MURS

PHIL FROST

AMANDA SEALES

MARC LaBELLE

136

SPANTO - BORN x RAISED - VENICE13

KAYA MARLEY

CHANEL WESTCOAST

LONO BRAZIL

JOHNNY OSBOURNE

RYAN MᶜGINNESS

JASON NOTO

RONNIE COOKE NEWHOUSE

THEODORE DIXON

TIMOTHY CURTIS - AGUA

KILLER MIKE

MAX GLAZER

DAVID BYRNE

DAVID "SHADI" PEREZ

150

ERIC ELMS

LUNA

152

EARL SWEATSHIRT

CHIP QUIGLEY

TYSON TOUSSANT
MARCELLA LEEDS

DJ SOUL
WILL DZOMBAK

HARLEY ADDISON
SET FREE

SKY GELLATLY
IAN DOYLE

156

NIGO®

PHARRELL WILLIAMS

JERRY WONDER

ROB JEST

TABATHA MᶜGURR

ACTION BRONSON

162

JULIETTE LEWIS

GEORGE DRAKOULIAS

MISTER MORT

HARLEY FLANAGAN

A.$.A.P. ROCKY

AI SHIMATSU

ANDRE PINARD BRICC BABY

ADRIAN MILES JOHN DALEY

DEAN & GIA COPPOLA RENE & GEMMA COPPOLA

STUART GRAHAM ALMA LACOUR

BOBBY HUNDREDS

A-TRAK

KRISTEN KISH

VIRGIL ABLOH

JANETTE BECKMAN

JOEY BADA$$

JR

MINYA OH - MISS INFO

MADCHILD

KAWAN "KP" PRATHER

RYAN TANNER

SCOOP DeVILLE

KEVIN McMULLAN

KAMAL GRAY

ROBERT "FROG" MENDOZA

MARK ANTHONY GREEN

ERIC BLAMOVILLE SYMONE MABRY

JAVANA MUNDY FERRIS BUELLER

WIZ KHALIFA

SELINA COLON

LOIC VILLEPONTOUX

LEWIS HAMILTON

KENNY SCHARF

METTE TOWLEY

MIKE LARSON

RICKY POWELL

RICARDO JACKSON

AYE HASEGAWA

DAO-YI CHOW

PETER MILLER

MICHAEL CAMARGO - UPSCALE VANDAL BRYA UNDERWOOD

ZACHARY ZELDIN BEN SMITH

KEHINDE HASSAN

TREIS HILL

TAIWO HASSAN

BRENT PASCHKE

SHEEK LOUCH

EVIDENCE

XZIBIT

STEVE "ESPO" POWERS

202

BAHR BROWN

FABOLOUS

STYLES P

CHAD HUGO

NIGEL SYLVESTER

BRICK STOWELL

ALEXANDRA DePERSIA

PLAIN PAT

APRIL McDANIELS

ED SHEERAN

MISTER ZONE

BEN SOLOMON

DREW COLEMAN

TEYANA TAYLOR

COREY SHAPIRO

CHRISTINA CHANDLER

13TH WITNESS

213

WALSHY FIRE

GWEN STEFANI

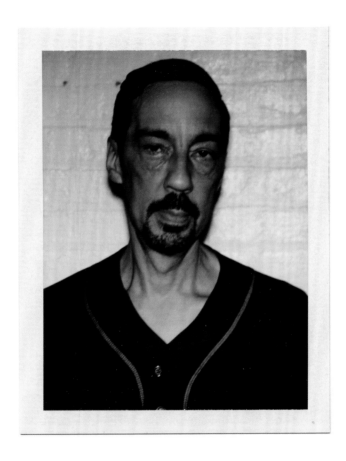

FUTURA

JACKIE HOLLAND

JASON GOLDWATCH

RITA ORA

TWO DOLLAR STEVE

BECK

DANASIA SUTTON

222

SEAN C

223

COREY EDNESS
RUFFY LEEDS

CHAKA ZULU
TAK

ALEXANDER SPIT KALEN HOLLOMON
JAMES POYSER JORDAN PAYTON

DOMINIQUE MALDONADO

SAGAN LOCKHART

NASTY BOY JASPER

$HERRY COSOVIC

THEODORE LEEDS

NAOMI CAMPBELL

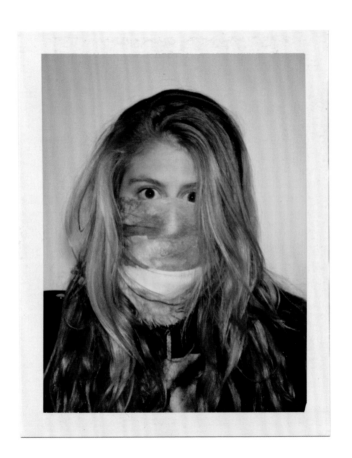

AUSTYN WEINER

BOW WOW

234

TANISHA SCOTT

JASON PINSKY

HIT BOY

SARAH COLETTE

MAC MILLER

PALOMA FAITH

ROCKY XU EVIE NO-MADDZ

MICELLE CARTER BT ROCKWELL

KYAMBO "HIP HOP" JOHNSON

BEA TALPLACIDO

LISA CHU

CASEY VEGGIES

STATIK SELEKTAH

243

MIKE GIANT

ROY CHOI

MAYOR

246

EMILY ROSE

88 KEYS

JOHN GIDDINGS

MR. LEN - COMPANY FLOW

BOLDY JAMES

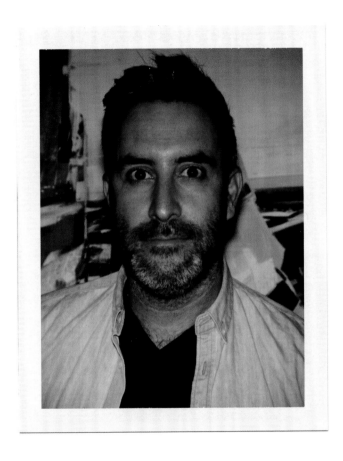

MICHAEL KAGAN

SIOBHAN BOYLE BEN YEFET
BRANDON ROSENBLATT HILTON "DEUCE" WRIGHT

BUDDY
DIEGO MOSCOSO

BOI 1DA
JOE BMW

254

MIKE SCHNAPP

"AJ" SOUR DIESEL

BRENNAN RABB

WILLIAM YAN

DON C

DICE THE GOD

JUS SKE

HAWAII MIKE

KRONDON

LATRELLE "MUNCHIE" SIMMONS

LENNY S

MARC BALET

KEVIN POON

MAXINE ASHLEY

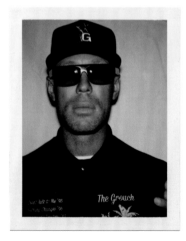

JOHN EMCH LOLA COLEMAN

THE GROUCH JAMES MAY

DENIS IDERMAN

LESLIE GREENE

REGINALD SYLVESTER II

RYAN POTESTA

JOSH FRANKLIN - MR. STASH

ANWAR CARROTS

OMARI HARDWICK

SHEP GORDON

ROHAN MARLEY

ROB STONE

SYD THA KYD

TACO OFWGKTA

DREW STONE

SHELDON SHEPARD

CHANCE LORD

RICHIE AKIVA

CHERYL DUNN

DEIRDRE MALONEY

BILLY LEVY

STEVE MARTINEZ

LAURA HILL FLANAGAN

CHRISTIAN MARTINEZ

CEY ADAMS

JILLIONAIRE

YUNA

WYATT NEUMANN

NATE RUESS

FAB 5 FREDDY

NOAH CALLAHAN-BEVER

SUE TSAI

MISHA LOUY DREA DE MATTEO

CODY BURKE JOHN GRAY

KATE ROSEN

DJ MARLON B

PHAROAH WILLIAMS

AVIVA YAEL

SHAWN "PECAS" COSTNER

SAMANTHA RONSON

ARJAN ROSKAM

JAHPHET NEGAST LANDIS - ROOFEO

DANIEL ARSHAM

BUN B

CHARLOTTE RONSON

AB LIVA

AMANDA SILVERMAN

MICKEY BOARDMAN